Meditations on the Republic

from the Vanity Toombs
Chronicles Vol. 1

(Portions written in the slave vernacular
of the Antebellum South)

Poetry by
Ruth Ann Kirton

Po-Cat and Peasant Publishing, Inc. - Bronxville, New York

Meditations on the Republic

from the Vanity Toombs Chronicles Vol. 1

Poetry by Ruth Ann Kirton

SPECIAL EDITION – JULY 4, 2012

PRINTED IN THE U.S.A. ⊜ GREAT BRITAIN ⊜ CONTINENTAL EUROPE

Coming Soon!

Also by Ruth Ann Kirton

Soon to be available at http://www.amazon.com; at Bookstores and Online Retailers; at Libraries and Academic Institutions; on Kindle enabled devices; at CreateSpace Direct; at our CreateSpace e-store at http://www.po-catandpeasantpublishinginc.net and at http://www.po-catandpeasant publishinginc.mobi.

September Miracle

A romantic thriller worthy of the 21st century, from the Vanity Toombs Chronicles Vol. 2

For an excerpt from the novel *September Miracle* turn to the back of this book.

Po-Cat and Peasant Publishing, Inc.
Bronxville, New York

DEDICATION

FOR GEORGIA ELLA COLEMAN

This book is dedicated to the memory of my hero and foster mother, Georgia Ella Coleman, who took me in at almost ten years old, taught me to read, to love, to live, and introduced me to poetry. I live to do the same for another…

ACKNOWLEDGMENT

I would like to give a special acknowledgement and thank-you to my Developmental Editor, Professor Doris Jackson, for lending her editing talents to this endeavor.

HEROES RUSH-IN
TO ALL WHO HAVE COME BEFORE
TO ALL WHO WILL COME AFTER
THANK-YOU

RAK

Meditations on the Republic

Poem Titles:

- Meditations on the Republic (part 1)
- Too deep for me (part 1)
- When we gonna be free?
- Po Po sure don't like me
- If a black man can't Pee Pee without being seen is he free?
- When I gits the Blues the Blues hallar back at me
- If Genius is a good thing, why they keep killing them off?
- Too deep for me (part 2)
- Meditation on being played in a very great way, Meditation on being Pimped all day
- Is this a con-spiracy?

+To tell the T-Ruth

+Sneaking and Peeking, Lying, Lynching,
   Cheating, Stealing, Murdering, Swindling,
   and Racketeering for them and they folks!
   Is that ok in a Democracy today?

+The American Way

+Why the Black Peoples are
   still in the Ghetto

+Peasants and Po-Cats

+What's left to overcome?
   ...dumb di, dumb di, da bull,
   "Dum Diversas"...!

+I be's compelled to say
   what I gots to say

+They be's compelled to do
   what they gots to do

+Meditations on the Republic (part 2)

MEDITATIONS

ON THE

REPUBLIC

Meditations on the Republic

(Part 1)

Meditations on the Republic:

It's already stolen it's already gone

When you are part of the group

that's not part of the group

What you got ain't yours to have

What you create ain't yours to hold

Before you get a chance to put your

brand-name on it

Government officials have already

virtual-tweaked it, creeped it

put it on sale in the virtual-world

under their name to bring them

fortune and fame

Your product sold for their

personal-gain

Stolen from your home for the

aggrandizement of your government

officials' homes

In this state of much duress poor

Americans try to do their best

Where might makes right it's called

the way of National Socialism

in this fatherland today

Liberty an idea that has seen its day

Equality, justice nay, they say

It's already stolen it's already gone

National Socialism on display

The Republic done the Democratic

Socialists' way

The Revolution was not

consented to or advised

National Socialism was virtually, just

brought into po-folks lives

Too deep for me
(Part 1)

Too deep for me

The Red scare

The Red fear

Too deep for me

The Red Communism

That hangs in the air

Too deep for me

But then I never was

Politically astute

Too deep for me

Every party's got its Shute

Too deep for me

'Cause I'm too easily duped

Eat, drink, and be merry

They say, they say

Do it, do it the hedonistic way

Don't worry about today

Tomorrow you'll pay

Too deep for me

The Red scare

The Red Fear

Too deep for me

The Red Communism

That hangs in the air

Too deep for me

The fear of God is what I fear

The beginning of wisdom

Is what I hear

When we gonna be free?

Some folks compelled
to keep gates
Some folks compelled
to be free
Some folks' life just
ain't worth livin'
lessen they ownin' me
That what make me ask
when we gonna be free?
Seem to me we ain't never
gonna be free
Lessen some folks stop being
compelled to keep gates

And some other folks stop

being compelled to keep hate

I ain't mentioning no names

Can't tell masters what they

already know

21st century done come

and be gone b/4 us know

Seem like a life sentence to me

this kind of slavery

When we gonna be free?

Must be the **MONEY!**

Po Po sure don't like me

Po Po sure don't like me
And they proud of it
Po Po sure don't like me
Then again a dog ain't never
liked a bone that wasn't free
Po Po sure don't like me
Can't! Got to keep they
emotional distance from
they victims you see
Po Po sure don't like me
And they proud of it they say

If a black man can't Pee Pee without being seen is he free?

I know a black man who can't
Pee Pee without being seen,
he's a money changer down at
the church
And I be asking myself
does that mean he not free
Can't tell by him he be walking
round all puffed up acting all free
But I says to myself he can't
Pee Pee without being seen
To me that mean he ain't free
But that black man don't mind the
sickness of being seen while he Pee

He don't see things the way I do
Think he too mean
He likes the sickness he say
As long as we women folks can't
do-do without being seen
he knows he be free
As long as him and his neighbors
can watch, they agree
If they have to transform us ladies
into whores, it's the price they
willing to have all us women folks
pay so the black man can be free in
the Community
But still I ask, is the black man
really free, can he be that naïve?

Sound like he a hypocrite to me! How can the black man be free if "We" ain't free? The whole thing is very creepy to me!

When I gits the Blues the Blues hallar back at me

When I gits the Blues

The Blues hallar back at me

When I gits the Blues

The Blues be saying

You can't have the Blues

Lessen you come see me

When I gits the Blues

The Blues hallar back at me

With a thump and a bump

Oops upside my head

When I gits the Blues

The Blues gits me

When I gits the Blues

The Blues hallar back at me
When I gits the Blues
The Blues gits hap-py
Hallar! Haller! Haller back at me
The Blues be saying
Yo', don't you want the key
When you git the Blues
The Blues can set you free
For a nickel, for a dime
You can be free all the time
Thump Thump, Thump Bump
I knows you heard the rhyme
When I gits the Blues
For a nickel, for a dime
The Blues be all mine

If Genius is a good thing, why they keep killing them off?

If genius is a good thing why they get so excited that they blood lust start a rising and the geniuses got to go in hiding?

If genius is a good thing why they keep killing them off before they can find a cure for cancer, how stop hunger and feed the world?

If genius is a good thing why the evil geniuses always able to get a little assist, if the price is right, with putting an end to the good geniuses b/4 they do all of they genius stuff?

If good genius is a good thing why
the evil geniuses always killing them
off?
No wonder ain't many black geniuses
in the world today!

Too deep for me
(part 2)

Too deep for me

The Red scare

The Red fear

Too deep for me

The Red Communism

That hangs in the air

Too deep for me

But I must be strong

I must bear the persecution

That hangs in air

For as the sirens blow the black

men at work outside my window

shut-up in fear and reverence

because they know some poor soul
is on his way to the place the
brothers go
Too deep for me
The Red scare
The Red Fear
Too deep for me
The Red Communism
That hangs in the air
Too deep for me
The fear of man is
The beginning of slavery
Too deep for me
The Socialist would have it
no other way
Too deep for me, for this they pray

Meditation on being played in a very great way, Meditation on being Pimped all day

Nothing like being played

in a very great way

Nothing like being played

and Pimped all day

Pimp got his hand in my pocket

Taking pennies by the millions

fo-sure, fo-sure, he above the law

Pimp making money off my name

in the name of Pimp-law,

'cause he need to score

Pimp jumping into my life

deciding my body can be every

man's whore, under penalty
of Pimp-law
Nothing like being played
in a very great way
Nothing like being played
and Pimped all day
Pimp got a woman
He got to pay to get laid
Pimp say that's why he got
his hand in my pocket 24/7 a day
Pimp say he got babies
he got to make
Pimp say him having children
changes everything
I say ok, but what that got to do
with me?

Pimp say I should understand
it mean I got to pay
for him and his children to be free
I say that don't sound right
is he fo-sure, is that the law?
Pimp say I am missing the point
Pimp say it is what it is
It ain't right it ain't wrong
It's just Pimp-law and by the way
he need more
I say I got my own babies
I want to make and I want to
leave them my money one day
Pimp say that's not his problem
Never was, nevermore

Pimp say he'll take my babies
to help him make more
Said he'll take my whole family
and my cat too, to make his score
I say that's cold-blooded, then I say
some more...
Nothing like being played
in a very great way
Nothing like being played
and Pimped all day
Nothing like being played
in the name of Pimp-law
Being played like that should be
against the law, would be if there
was justice for all, fo-sure, fo-sure

Is this a con-spiracy?

Is this a con-spiracy

Or did absolute power

stop corrupting, absolutely?

Ain't nothing changed in the psyche

of man in 10,000 years

Which means absolute power

still corrupts absolutely today

So yeah this is a con-spiracy

The con is the notion of change

When everybody knows the more

things change the more

they stay absolutely the same

Yes the more things change the more

they stay absolutely the same

When they talk about change

They just jerking your chain

That's the real con-spiracy

Every dollar in your pocket they say

got their family-name on it

But, just to be nice they say maybe

they'll have one of their sons throw

a penny back at 'cha for change

Hum, yup yup it's a con-spiracy

To tell the T-Ruth

To tell the T-Ruth to Ruth

would bring her fortune and fame

To tell the T-Ruth to Ruth

would ease her pain

To tell the T-Ruth to Ruth

would honor her name

To tell the T-Ruth to Ruth

would end the game

They could no longer scapegoat

and scandalize Ruth's name

Then where would the

desperados be?

They would be lost in

their own obscurity!

Sneaking and Peeking, Lying, Lynching, Cheating, Stealing, Murdering, Swindling, and Racketeering for them and they folks! Is that ok in a Democracy today?

Today in this country the judges say it's ok for folks to sneak and peek, lie, lynch, cheat, steal, murder, swindle, and racketeer with the heat, so they folks can git made and be paid in this socialized-economy today

Just like back in the days of the Picnic-lynching and hay, when it was ok, for some folks in this country to sneak and peek, lie, lynch, cheat, steal, murder, swindle, and racketeer for them and they folks

Today it's just not called prejudice or corruption it's been redefined and excused as elegant aggression by the judges

Which the judges say makes it ok, long as folks don't sneak and peek, lie, lynch, cheat, steal from, murder, swindle, and racketeer equals today

Long as they keep the social contract and don't break the gentleman's code, which is a binding agreement to sneak and peek, lie, lynch, cheat,

steal, murder, swindle, and racketeer
folks that ain't really folks, just
animals what the judges say

Them folks that still ain't part of the
binding social contract today, they
just part of the social order not
equal that way

Then it's ok in a Democracy today, in
order to keep the social order, just
like back in the days of the picnic-
lynching and hay

The judges say it's ok today, to train
black folks how to stay in they place
how to be sneaked and peeked, lied
to, lynched, cheated, stolen from,

murdered, swindled, and racketeered without having anything to say in their own defense, just like back in the days of slavery, Jim Crow, picnic-lynching and the reality of hay

If everybody is doing it in an elegantly aggressive way, the judges say, really, it's ok... they have decided, that in their learned opinion, that's the right way to keep black folks in their place today!

The American Way

My master thinks he can do
everything better than me
Which he says makes him
far more deserving than me
And because of what he thinks
my master he says
God told him he owns me
mind, body, and even my soul
God told him to hold me
My master he says it is not
my time to be set free
He says that would be
wrong for me
If it were the right time

he says honestly
he would tell me
Liberty he says is for those who
know what to do with it
Money he says is for those who are
allowed to use it
Property he says is for those
who can toll it
And black folks like me
he says is for him
to have and to hold it
What he says is
It's the American way, ok???

Why the Black Peoples are still in the Ghetto!

400 hundred years of blood,

sweat, and tears

400 hundred years and still got fears

400 hundred years plus another

hundred of being "free"

Why the black peoples are still in the

ghetto?

Well, it beats me!

Peasants and Po-Cats

Peasants and Po-Cats been silenced
and can't have no say lessen they
want the Po Po up in they face
telling them just what to say

Peasants and Po-Cats been shown
the way it's gonna be in this 21st
century of days

Peasants and Po-Cats been silenced I
say their protectors traded in they
rights for big bank accounts and to
git paid

Sold to the highest bidder, with a little hustle and flow as the gift that keeps on giving, what they call black gold and it don't ever git old

Peasants and Po-Cats ain't got nothing to say, Yup Yup, Yup Yup, they been silenced today and da rich man ain't got no complaints

What's left to overcome?
...dumb di, dumb di, da bull "Dum Diversas"...!

Da man say you be a crazy niggra
if'in you thinkin' there be something
left to overcome

dumb di, dumb di, da bull "dum
diversas", dumb di, dumb di, da dumb

Da man say just be a happy niggra
and he give you permission to pray

dumb di, dumb di, da bull "dum
diversas", dumb di, dumb di, da dumb

Da man say stop all this crazy talk
about your rights and your say

dumb di, dumb di, da bull "dum
diversas", dumb di, dumb di, da dumb

Da man say you be a dead niggra if'in
you don't do what he say

dumb di, dumb di, da bull "dum
diversas", dumb di, dumb di, da dumb

Da man say shut your mouth and pay
for the things da man do and say

dumb di, dumb di, da bull "dum
diversas", dumb di, dumb di, da dumb

Da man say what's left for a niggra
to overcome? Nothing! Da man say

dumb di, dumb di, da bull "dum
diversas", dumb di, dumb di, da dumb

Now go on out there and play God
wants it that way

dumb di, dumb di, da bull "dum diversas[1]", dumb di, dumb di, da dumb {...} pray niggra, pray, pray, pray!

1. The papal bull "Dum Diversas" of 1452 was issued by Pope Nicholas V in Rome and read "We grant you [Kings of Spain and Portugal] by these present document, with our Apostolic Authority, full and free permission to invade, search out, capture, and subjugate the Saracens {...} wherever they may be, as well as their kingdoms, duchies, counties, principalities, and property {...} and to reduce their persons into perpetual slavery." (retrieved from http://www.wikipedia.org Categories: 1452 works | 15th century in Portugal | Documents of Pope Nicholas V | Slave trade | 15th-century papal bulls.)

This logic was eventually used to justify the enslavement of all African peoples of color, particularly the blacks because they were thought of as animals and savages.

I be's compelled to say
what I gots to say

I be's compelled to say

what I gots to say

I learned how to do that

way back in the day

Listening to the black poets

brought me along the way

Now today I be's compelled to say

what I gots to say

Can't nothing on earth

take that gift away

Whatever the price

I gots to have my say

Compelled I am

Compelled I say

Compelled to say

what this Po-Cat gots to say

Compelled by forces near

Compelled by forces far

Compelled by forces I hear

close to my heart

I be's compelled to say

what I gots to say

They be's compelled to do what they gots to do

They be's compelled to do
what they gots to do
And taking care-of-business
is what they do well
Can't no one git around
the spell they compel
Dead or alive
how they works they evil jive
Talking smack like a hack
don't work where they at
Big talk got to walk
They creed is of greed

and they gots they needs
Taking-care-of-business
is they beast-of-burden they
use to feed they greed
with they evil deeds
For skulls and bones they be's
compelled to do
what they gots to do
They men of action
So don't you be no fool
If they'd do it to me
They'd do it to you
Taking-care-of-business
is what they do
Don't you be duped
with the dead

with the alive

how they works they evil jive

It is how they beguile

with lying, cheating,

sneaking, peeking,

stealing, slaying,

hardly paying

They be's compelled to do

what they gots to do

Meditations on the Republic (part 2)

Meditations on the Republic:

It's already stolen it's already gone

When you are part of the group

that's not part of the group

What you got ain't yours to have

What you create ain't yours to hold

It's already stolen it's already gone

Sold to da man who bought your

right to a life and a happy home

Liberty and justice for all

Nay they say what's the big idea

Everybody ain't equal

Didn't you hear

'de triumph of 'de will

'de manifestation of 'de ego

'de snatching of 'de soul

'de theft of 'de Blueberry Pie

'de Pink Elephant in 'de room

makes no proclamations

National Socialism on display

The Republic done the

Democratic Socialists' way

Meditations on the Republic:

Jumped into our lives, set up a

global display of families broken by

Government-Royalty today

Not wise to fight when might

makes right just another one...

Americans shall overcome!

About the Author

Ruth Ann Kirton, a native New Yorker, attended Iona College in New Rochelle, New York. She graduated with a Bachelors of Arts Degree in Philosophy, Phi Sigma Tau honors, a Concentration in Business Administration, and a Minor in History. In her senior year, she was nominated by Iona College's administration to represent the school in the nation's Outstanding Young American competition, an honor she cherishes to this day.

The author's amateur journalism career began as a Staff Writer for the Ionian Newspaper's Features Department, writing weekly articles for the Iona audience. She also gained public speaking experience as a team-member and President of Iona's Parliamentary Debate Team, the Lannon Forensic Council, and as a Senior Representative to Iona College's Student Government Association. She was chosen for the Iona College Mentorship program, an honor given each year to a limited number of students during their senior year.

Ruth Ann has spent many years working in the public sector and corporate America, using the skills she acquired during her years of study at Iona College. Ruth Ann was Georgia Ella Coleman's (Nana's) first foster child to graduate from college, for which she is very proud. She is forever in debt to the Coleman family for helping her complete the task and to Nana for being the first person to believe that she would one day be a published Poet. The publication of her debut book of poetry, Meditations on the Republic is a wonderful accomplishment for Ruth Ann Kirton. It is her first published book of record and is available at http://www.amazon.com; at Bookstores and Online Retailers; at Libraries and Academic Institutions; on Kindle enabled devices; at CreateSpace Direct; at our CreateSpace e-store at http://www.po-catandpeasantpublishinginc.net and at http://www.po-catandpeasantpublishinginc.mobi.

Ruth Ann would like to offer a special thanks to all of the Poets, Writers, and Philosophers who came before her and inspired her by sharing the gift of their wisdom with all of us.

READ AN EXCERPT FROM THE NOVEL

September Miracle

A romantic thriller worthy of the 21ˢᵗ century

By Ruth Ann Kirton

from the Vanity Toombs Chronicles, Vol. 2
Po-Cat and Peasant Publishing, Inc.
Bronxville, New York

Soon to be available at http://www.amazon.com; at Bookstores and Online Retailers; at Libraries and Academic Institutions; on Kindle enabled devices; at CreateSpace Direct; at our CreateSpace e-store at http://www.po-catandpeasantpublishinginc.net and at http://www.po-catandpeasant publishinginc.mobi.

PROLOGUE

If I said that soul mates exist and that a person can find hers, I would be believed? But if I said that Knights in Shining Armor exist and one day one will come knocking at the door, I would have a good chance of being told that they only exist in fairy tales and romance novels. If I persisted and said no, it is true, for I actually met one; I would probably be asked what drug I was on when this wondrous occasion took place.

Nevertheless, I am here to say that in this modern age of the 21st century, Knights in Shining Armor do exist and this is the story of one such Knight and the woman he loves. I share this story, particularly with young women, because I have been informed that within the population of today's men a large portion of them have been raised to be Knights in Shining Armor. I wanted to get the word out to all the young women out there who have been told to give up on their dreams of ever finding their Knights in Shining Armor, do not give up. There is a chance that he may still come knocking at the door one day.

My advice to a young woman having a hard time finding her Knight in Shining Armor is, rather than giving up, losing faith, and settling for less, take off the blinders so that when he appears again, he can be seen. It would be a wonderful thing to marry a soul mate who is also a Knight in Shining Armor, rather than just marrying a soul mate, or a man one was in love with at the time of the wedding! Think of how low the divorce rate would go in this country if more women married her Knight in Shining Armor!

So here is the story. The peculiar part about it is that this Knight showed up in the most unusual of places in all of America -- Corporate America. That is how Knights are these days it seems! They show up where they are least expected. So remember to keep those eyes open.

Who am I? I am Debbie (Vanity) Toombs, the Hicks' family historian, keeper of the Hicks Family Diary, a freelance reporter, writer, poet and artist with much "divatude". I am also the cousin of the woman who found her Knight in Shining Armor. In other words, I am the one with the 411. I am the one who got the story...

Conversation between two friends:

"Gerry, have you ever heard of someone feeling high after being kissed. I felt lightheaded and dizzy after Jim kissed me. Do you have a scientific explanation for that?"

"Did you eat today, Keisha?"

"Yeah, it wasn't from not eating; it was as if I had tasted the nectar of the gods, drunk sweet wine. His lips were so divine."

"Girl, you just sound like you're in love; that's the only scientific explanation I have."

"No, but, Gerry, he set off a chemical reaction in me; I had to lie down for a while before I had the strength to call you, and I'm still not over it. I have all of this energy flowing through my body; it's like he filled me with his life force, but it's not an orgasmic feeling. There must be another name for it. I'm intoxicated with life!"

"Again, with the chemical reactions between you two, I don't know, child; I never experienced anything like what you described without some alcoholic beverage being involved; you'd have to talk to a sexologist. All I can say is if that's what his kisses do to you, can you imagine what will happen when he really puts something on you? He's going to send you to the moon and back, stratosphere baby. You're not going to know what hit you. He'll have to call a doctor to revive you."

"It's not going to be that bad, Gerry."

"No, it's going to be that good. Love makes the greatest lovers; that much I know from experience."

"Well he is like no man I've ever been with. Where Kevin used to suckle and feast, and I thought that was something special, Jim devours me."

"Girl in a year you won't even remember Kevin's last name. In two years you'll be referring to Kevin as that guy I used to go out with."

"And, Gerry, when Jim kisses me, he trembles in my arms. I could just die, between the passion, the love, his whispering my name, the devouring me, the sweet nectar of his lips, and his trembling in my arms with desire for me, I'm whipped. For once, I feel like I'm sitting down to the banquet table."

"And, he's whipped, too. That's what I'm talking about," Gerry said. "All of that is happening in a kiss. You are making him tremble in your arms girl; right there you know you have a man who thinks that you have the pot of gold. And, that's how it should be. I'm just saying, he's going to be the great love of your life if you would only open yourself to the possibility."

Gerry continued, "That's what I try to tell these women out here, but they don't listen to me because I'm a gay black man. Black women today keep running behind these trifling black men who think the man has the pot of gold. They value themselves way above any black woman they are with and treat them like whores, pimping, and carrying on, in and out of all kinds of women's beds. The women can't control their men these days. So I tell them you need to expand your horizons; there are men out there who are willing to treat you like black gold, and if I were a woman, I wouldn't tolerate the garbage some men be dishing out to you sisters for a second. I'm an Old-School-Fool; I demand respect. But they tell me straight-up; you're not a woman, and you don't know what it's like out here. Competition is steep; you have to take what you can get. Chivalry is dead now if it was ever alive in the black ghetto. They claim they ain't waiting for no gallant Knight in Shining Armor to come riding in on his high horse; they just lucky if they can find a for-real black man. Sad isn't it, to have such low expectations of love and life?"

"Anyway, so I say good-luck and let it go, child, because I am not about to explain to every woman I talk to how I'm an effeminate man; I have more female hormones than male, and I almost know exactly what it's like to be a black woman. After all I'm just trying to help a po-cat out, if I can't do that without bearing my soul to every Tammy, Deborah, and Jane I meet, then too bad."

"Got-cha Gerry, self-preservation is rule #1 in all situations. Live to fight another day, as they say. You want to be there to help the next person out. Maybe they will be more receptive to your message."

"You got that straight, baby-girl."

"Gerry, I hope you know how appreciative I am of all the help you've given me with Jim; even if I haven't changed overnight, I still love you for trying to help me see the light and not miss out on a good thing."

"I know you appreciate it, baby-girl. I know you'll come around sooner or later, and if you don't, maybe it just wasn't meant to be no matter how good Jim makes you feel. Sometimes that's just how things work out. Life is a journey; all we can do is take the trip and hope we have a little fun along the way. But one thing's for sure life is a trip."

"You got that right, Gerry!"

Three day's later:

"Save something for your husband," Nana II would say whenever she gave Keisha advice about how to prepare for marriage. Those words pounded in Keisha's ears as she put on her little black dress to get ready for her date with Jim. She wondered if Nana II would roll over in her grave if she found out that the potential husband she had saved something for was a white man. She hoped she wasn't cursing the memory of her favorite Nana by accidentally falling in love with a Caucasian.

As she slipped on her black and red pumps, she remembered how Nana II always tried to deny any white lineage on her side of the family and was proud that she had married her great-grand father, great-grandpa Moses Aaron Hicks, the blackest man she could find in North Carolina. Nana II always said, "The blacker the berry the sweeter the juice."

As Keisha applied the finishing touches of her make-up and her black-cherry lipstick, she thought about the mystery that surrounded the untold story of Nana II's mother's mother and how Nana II, Georgia Charlotte Campbell-Hicks, would always change the subject anytime her great-grand daughter would try to piece her family history together. The most Keisha could gather was that her great-grand mother's, grand-mother had been a slave and that Nana II did not get her fair skin, wavy hair, and light eyes from any lineage on the master's side.

Nana II had said in so many words that her grandmother would have died before she let a white man rape her or force her into a lifelong role of Jezebel, paramour, whore, or mother-of-master's-children that she knew were going to be relegated to the caste of slave and the status of peasantry in their own father's house. No, Nana II explained that what had happened was that she had Indian blood in her on her grandmother's side, and that was where she got her fair skin, wavy hair, and light eyes. She went to her grave insisting that her lineage was more black than anything else; the implication was that consenting adults even during slavery had conceived all of Keisha's generations in love.

Nana II tried to lead Keisha to believe that her family had escaped the unfortunate period in black history, when during slavery black women were forced into sexual relationships with their masters to produce off-spring that could be sold and maintained in slavery perpetually to increase their daddy's/master's wealth, a practice that became increasingly more necessary after the importation of slaves from Africa was outlawed by Congress. And, after the sixth President of the U.S.A., John Quincy Adams, won the Amistad Supreme Court Case which moved the government to enforce Congress' law banning the importation of slaves from Africa by penalizing slave traffickers who continued to bring African born slaves into this country, the case relegated them to the status of terrorists, engaged in acts of war against sovereign nations and criminals of war who committed crimes against the free peoples of those nations.

Nana II and great-grandpa Moses went to extra lengths to instill a sense of worth in their off-spring, as a result of struggling through what they referred to as the on-going dark-ages in black history, that were worse than the Medieval days of European history, matched only by the Jewish Holocaust brought on by the mass psychosis and lunacy spread by Adolf Hitler's take-over of the German Worker's Political Party; his evolving it into the National Socialist German Worker's Political Party's 13-year regime also known as the Nazi Party; his take-over of Germany's SA and turning it into the Nazi SS the military forces of Nazi Germany's Third Reich – whose chant was "One People One Realm"; his creation of the hatemongering Ministry of Propaganda to sell hate by using prominent German Actors and Actresses to be spokespersons for the spread of hate, white supremacy, and the mass psychosis hate-thinking breeds; his creation of the Gestapo (secret state Police/terroristic gang of Aryan-henchmen), all of whose combined forces led to the Jewish Holocaust, WWII, and the killing of 50 million people worldwide. Adolf Hitler and the criminal form of government he created known as National Socialism were free to commit heinous atrocities and crimes against humanity in the name of the Aryan Nuremberg Laws and for the goal of world domination during their reign of terror at the cost of the rest of the world's Human Rights.

The great-gramps filled in the gaps in Nana II's own family history with references to the greater black race at large and periods in black history where the people overcame great adversity, exploitation, and oppression. They reminded Keisha that great-grandpa Moses' family history could be traced back to the blacks that fought with Crispus Attucks, the first man to lose his life in the American Revolutionary War, to free the colonies from the tyranny of King George III. They reminded Keisha that it was the combined effort of whites and blacks that fought for freedom from tyranny that gained the Colonies the independence they needed to write the American Constitution and set up the first government in the history of mankind that gave the hope of equality to all that reached its shores. She learned that some of great-grandpa Moses' ancestors were amongst the first free-blacks in America, managing to earn their freedom long before the Civil War freed blacks from slavery.

In the early days of their marriage, great-grandpa Moses tried to get Nana II to let go of her shame about slavery, without much avail, so he joined her in refocusing the gaps in her history to the history of the greater black race at-large. For instance, when Keisha would ask Nana II and great-grandpa Moses what kind of Indian blood Nana II had in her, they would both change the subject and say, "It didn't matter 'cause she's black and that's what's important to "folks" in this world today." Then they would start talking about popular heroes such as Henry Blair, the first person of color to receive a patent in the U.S.A., Elijah (The real McCoy) McCoy and his 42 inventions, Howard Latimer and his work with Alexander Graham Bell and Thomas Edison, Benjamin Banneker and the White House, Frederick Jones and his World War II portable cooling units, Edmond Berger and his Spark

Plugs, Otis Boykin and Pace Makers, George Washington Carver and peanut butter, Charles Brooks and Street Sweeper Trucks, and O.S. Williams and the Apollo Moon landings and beyond.

They would carry on this way, telling Keisha about the various contributions black people had made to this country and to the world while avoiding a discussion of Nana II's possible white lineage and the shame slave women carried and passed on to their daughters as a result of the degrading sacrifices they had to make to survive slavery at the hands of white men. Nana II and great-grandpa Moses wanted to break the cycle in their family and others. As the only free men, white men gave themselves the right to oppress and exploit black women at their master's personal discretion and will. Slaves survived as human-chattel at their master's pleasure/choice. White men gave themselves the right to treat them inhumanely and contemptuously; the practice continued under Jim Crow, Anti-miscegenation laws, the Racial Integrity Act, and beyond. As Keisha sprayed some Obsession perfume on her neck and down her cleavage, she reminisced about how her great-gramps seemed to make sure that by the time they finished giving her a real history lesson, it was usually time for dinner or for her to get off the phone or some such thing. She reflected on how blessed she was to have had the opportunity to get to know her great-grand parents before they passed.

Great-grandpa Moses and Nana II found each other in a system that oppressed and exploited black families while forcibly denying blacks their most basic right, the right to be a human being. They created a bond that kept their humanity alive, while overwhelming forces tried to extinguish it. For Keisha they hoped that she would be part of a generation of blacks in America that finally succeeded in escaping the cycle of the master/slave, pimp/whore relationship that has defined black existence for centuries. They hoped instead that she would live a life redefined as the life lived by free human beings who are able to sit at the table with other human beings of all races, creeds, and colors as equals, living the American dream not the American nightmare.

Great-grandpa Moses and Nana II created what they called the Hicks Family Diary, and hoped it would pave a road to the American dream for their descendants and their people as they came up from slavery, oppression and exploitation. As a result, the successors of slave owners, the predecessors of Nazis, the American hatemongers, the Knights of the Ku Klux Klan who are obsessed with restoring the glory days of the antebellum south took an interest in the Hicks family and the diary. Klan-Crafters have made careers out of their efforts to destroy and/or confiscate everything the Hicks family has ever worked for in this country. Keisha knew this. She knew her family history well and all of the contributions her family made to this country and the black community, as chronicled in the Hicks Family Diary. She knew the struggles of her people and because of what she knew, by falling in love with Jim O'Neill, she knew others would question her choice.

Keisha smiled as she looked in the mirror at her own dark brown skin and eyes, naturally kinky hair with its perm and thought about how Nana II managed to return to her ancestors with the secret about her lineage intact. She also smiled that Nana II had managed to marry black enough to pretty much ensure that if there was any leftover shame passed down in her blood line from slavery, that hadn't been erased when Nana II looked in the mirror, it was certainly erased when her great-grand-daughter looked in the mirror.

Nana II had done well her job while she was in the land of the living or had she? All she had wanted out of life was to get rid of the shame of slavery. She had a dream and prayed God would have mercy and grant it. Nana II wanted her children to truly be "free at last." She taught her girl-children to always ask themselves the Sojourner Truth question – "Ar'n't I a Woman?" And, to make sure that the way they were being treated by the man in their life always meant that the answer was "yes" because in this world it mattered whether men thought of females as women or human-chattel.

As Keisha readied herself for Jim's arrival, she reflected on the history lessons from her great-gramps and wondered if she was "saving something" for the right man. Just as Keisha's brush stroked her hair for the last time, Jim O'Neill rang her doorbell. Keisha's heart leapt into her throat as she called out, "I'll be right there honey," and ran to the door.

www.ingramcontent.com/pod-product-compliance
Lightning Source LLC
Chambersburg PA
CBHW031332040426

42443CB00005B/307